HOW TO WHITTLE

The Taunton Press
Inspiration for hands-on living®

The Taunton Press, Inc.
63 South Main Street, PO Box 5506,
Newtown, CT 06470-5506
email: tp@taunton.com

This book was designed, conceived, and produced
by Quantum Books Ltd,
an imprint of The Quarto Group
6 Blundell Street
London N7 9BH
United Kingdom

Publisher: Kerry Enzor
Editorial: Charlotte Frost, Julia Shone, and
Emma Harverson
Production Manager: Rohana Yusof
Designers: Tokiko Morishima and Ros Saunders
Photographers: Josh Nava, Vic Phillips,
and Simon Pask

E-WHIT

Library of Congress Cataloging-in-Publication Data
in progress

ISBN 978-1-63186-891-7

Printed in China
10 9 8 7 6 5 4 3 2 1

Publisher's note: Woodworking can be danger
The tools used can cause serious injury, so exerc
extreme caution at all times. Always read the ins
manuals supplied with your equipment and use
safety guards and procedures recommended. Al
information and advice on methods and techni
given in this book are believed to be true and ac
However, neither the author nor the publisher c
accept any legal liability for errors or omissions.

Josh Nava

HOW TO WHITTLE

25 beautiful projects to carve by hand

The Taunton Press

CONTENTS

INTRODUCTION

WHITTLING HAS AN EASE of entry that something like building a table or cabinet does not. You do not need a workshop, machinery, or many tools, just two knives, a way to sharpen them, a small amount of wood, and some time. This means you could be at home and still work on a project, whether you are carving on the couch watching television or in the kitchen listening to music.

With a couple of knives and a handful of other tools, you enable yourself to make the things that you and your family use and need. These tools work like a set of keys, each unlocking a door for you to make things in a new way, with wood that is, of all things, free. A good folding saw can help turn a neighbor's tree trimmings, which are just waiting to be hauled to the dump, into a handful of cooking spoons. A few logs waiting to be split for the fireplace can be turned into a series of butter paddles.

Before the Industrial Revolution, farmers would sit down at the end of a long day gathered around the fire with their children. While they told stories, they would also carve something useful that they needed. This could be a new ladle for the cooking pot, stakes for the garden, a walking stick, or small toys for the children. The wood from a tree branch collected on the way home would be all the material that was needed for the task. The knife the farmer carved with was used all day for various chores, and as such was an extension of his body.

What you needed, you made, and you made it with the materials available to you within nature—a tree crook from an oak felled during a storm, or a piece of firewood that looked especially good set aside for carving. This can still be the case.

Our favorite items, our go-to's, carry an intuitive sense to them—a favorite mug, a well-worn shirt, or our grandmother's cooking spoon that still finds its place in preparing meals. Becoming aware of why some objects work so well and why others fail is to become aware of the language of design. When we speak this language, we can use bits and pieces of it to make long-lasting things of our own.

A well-made kitchen spoon can serve a friend for decades to come, and every time they use it, they will think of its origin, because it is imbued with your story. It is an object that is useful, meaningful, and comes from your own hands, made from materials that you gathered from nature. What could be more meaningful than that?

Whittling is great for learning about working wood and attuning our eye to subtlety of form and well-balanced design. It is a wonderful application of hands-on engineering, artistic expression, and perseverance. Within this book you will find the skills you need to start carving, beginning with the basic cuts and techniques before applying them to create a range of beautiful homewares, gifts, and keepsakes.

TECHNIQUES

CHOOSING YOUR WOOD

Trees are made up of massive bundles of long fibers running from the ground up the trunk and extending out to all the branches. Each bundle of fibers is used to transport nutrients and water, either up to the leaves for photosynthesis or down to the roots for storage. Each year trees build a new layer of these fibers that we commonly know as growth rings.

Fast-growing species will put on a very thick layer during the spring and a smaller, denser layer in late summer, resulting in softer wood throughout the tree; this is what we call "softwood." Other trees have a more even layering, resulting in less discernible rings when looking at a cross-section. Usually these close-grained "hardwoods" are the best kinds of woods to make tools for your kitchen.

GREEN WOOD VS. SEASONED WOOD

Green wood, or wet wood, is wood that comes from a freshly cut tree. Trees have an incredibly high moisture content, which makes them flexible and easy to carve while the moisture is still in the wood. Upon being cut, with the end grain exposed to the air, the moisture within the wood rapidly escapes. This causes cracking or "checking," as seen on the end of firewood. The wood of the tree is in tension, and as the moisture leaves, the fibers of the tree shrink and start to pull away from one another. In larger pieces of wood, like that used for furniture, the tension of the wood in combination with moisture loss results in major twisting or cracking.

In order to stabilize the wood and reduce this undesirable twisting and checking, the wood is "seasoned." This is done either by air-drying stacked boards under cover, or by placing them in a low-temperature kiln to evaporate most of the moisture from the wood, thereby hardening the lignin that gives wood its flexibility. This process makes wood very hard to work except by very sharp tools, often with power behind them.

For our purposes, it is best to avoid seasoned wood. This is not to say that you cannot carve seasoned wood; it just takes much longer and is harder on your tools. For most of the projects in this book I have worked with green wood, but if you must use seasoned wood, try to find softwoods that lend themselves better to carving.

1 Sycamore
2 Cherry
3 Black
   walnut
4 Cherry
5 Walnut
6 Cherry
7 Sycamore
8 Poplar
9 Ash
10 Hackberry

GOOD WOODS FOR CARVING

Learn the types of trees in your neighborhood and you can more readily identify good wood for whittling. Local tree identification books are often the first place to look and will be your best friend in this. However, you do not need to know the kind of tree a wood comes from in order to carve it. I still encounter woods that I cannot identify. Experimentation and the resulting experience will teach you if a wood is suitable for its purpose. Try anything green and pay attention to how it works.

Anything green

Even the very hardest of woods are actually quite easy to carve while they are still wet, which is a great advantage to the projects in this book. Cherry wood might feel like carving stone when it is dry, but while green it is closer to carving a hard pear or cheese. This means that wherever you are in the world, you have access to a wide variety of unique and interesting woods that might otherwise be impossible to work while dry.

Fruit woods

I do not have a fruit orchard near me, but if I did I would try to befriend the owner. Fruit trees such as apple, peach, pear, plum, lime, cherry, and many nut trees (walnut, almond, and so on) are wonderful to carve. Apple wood is smooth and easy to carve while it is green, and then dries to a hard and durable wood that is resistant to abuse, making it an excellent wood for kitchen tools like stirring and cooking spoons.

Other woods

Other fantastic woods to carve are birch, maple, holly, dogwood, and sycamore. Birch is an almost effortless wood to carve and dries to a beautiful pale color. You may have none or all of these woods near you, but again, find and experiment with what you do have as almost any wood will do.

A freshly cut log is easier to carve than seasoned wood. It is also cheaper to buy, with plenty of free sources if you use a little imagination.

WHERE TO FIND WOOD

While you can buy wood off the rack from your local home center, these are often seasoned woods and the cost can quickly add up. With a little imagination there are plenty of alternative places you can source quality wood cheaply or at no cost.

In the wild

My first source for carving material is a drive through local neighborhoods looking for someone who has recently trimmed their tree. This is where a portable folding saw becomes really useful. Keep one in your car and you will always be ready to grab that perfect crook of a tree or small section from a trunk at the roadside.

Fallen trees

Sometimes storms will take down trees or their branches, and this becomes a great source of wood if you can transport it. Obviously you will need to take care, as a tree hung up in surrounding trees can still be dangerous. Look for those that have made their way to the ground. A folding saw can be useful for smaller sections of trunk, depending on size, but otherwise you will need a chainsaw or a friend who owns one to help, which will result in a windfall of usable wood. If using a chainsaw, there is a whole list of safety precautions you need to be aware of, so be sure you know what you are doing and are exercising proper caution.

Tree trimmers and arborists

If you are a green wood worker, it would benefit you greatly to make friends with a local arborist. This can result in offcuts from big jobs of freshly cut pieces of old-growth trees. Most tree services and arborists are enlisted to dispose of trees either by hauling them away or chipping the trees up and disposing of them in a landfill. Sometimes you can do them a favor by helping them dispose of the tree via your usage.

Municipal waste sites

Because trees are biodegradable and high in carbon, many municipal waste sites separate out the branches and trees they receive from the trash. If you can find these places and get permission to glean, this can be a consistent source of usable woods for carving.

Home centers and hardwood dealers

If for some reason you do not have access to green wood or you are just eager to get started, you can go to your local home center and buy wood off the rack. This is going to be seasoned wood, meaning the wood has been dried in a kiln to prevent it from warping, rotting, or checking. The woods you find in a home center are primarily for building purposes, though you can find some "hobby" woods for the kinds of projects in this book.

If you are going to do this, I recommend pine, fir, cedar, and poplar. These woods are still relatively soft and will go easier on your tools. However, because they are dry, they are more prone to splitting while working. Oak, maple, and southern yellow pine are not great woods to carve unless you have access to power tools. It can be done, but your hands will feel it.

TOOLBOX

To get started, you only need three tools: a straight knife, a hook knife, and a hatchet. There are obviously more tools that you can acquire over time, but these three tools will enable you to make something from nothing in a vast number of ways.

CHOPPING BLOCK

When using a hatchet, you will need a wide, solid, and stable surface that will let you transfer the force of the hatchet cuts directly into the workpiece. This is where a chopping block becomes a workbench. At its simplest, the chopping block can be a slice of tree trunk 10–20 in. (25–50cm) in diameter and around knee height. This will allow you to comfortably hew wood while sitting. You can add legs to a chopping block that will allow you to stand while you work. If you wish to do this, I recommend three stout legs, as a three-legged stool can sit firmly on irregular ground.

KNIVES

When you think of the term "whittling," the first image that probably comes to mind is a pocketknife. You can carve wood with a sharp pocketknife, but there are much better and inexpensive knives that are more suited for this purpose.

The first is a straight-bladed knife with what is called a "Scandi" grind. A Scandi grind is a wide bevel that makes the cutting edge very thin and long. The benefits of this type of knife quickly become evident upon use—the knife allows you to cleanly carve smooth surfaces and get into tight corners with ease. This straight knife is used for straight cuts and outside curves. You will become very familiar with this knife, as it will do the majority of the work. The best and simplest of these knives to get hold of is a Mora knife. From there you can find specialty makers with specialty price points.

The second type of knife you need is a hook knife. This knife has a curved blade that will allow you to

1 Hatchet
2 Axe
3 Straight "Scandi" knife
4 Hook knife
5 Folding saw

carve the hollowed-out bowls of spoons, cups, and dishes. Hook knives come in right- and left-handed versions, so make sure you purchase the one that is appropriate for you. There also exists a blade that is both right- and left-handed, meaning there are sharpened edges along both sides of the curve. I do not recommend getting this knife, as there will be times when you want to push on the back edge of the hook knife with your opposite thumb. Again, Mora knives are the best introductory route.

A portable folding saw is ideal for cutting up any wood you find by the roadside.

AXES OR HATCHETS

The terms "axe" and "hatchet" often become interchangeable when talking about wood carving. Technically, a hatchet is a one-handed axe, and this is the kind that you need. Often these are called wildlife hatchets or carving axes, but either way you are looking for a hatchet with a handle 10–14 in. (25–35cm) long. Hatchets can be purchased new or you can search antique stores and flea markets for a good old one and give it new life by fitting a new handle (see page 77). Either way, make sure it is sharp and keep it clean, dry, and the edge protected.

SAWS

A good coarse-toothed folding or pruning saw is indispensable when harvesting wood. I say coarse-toothed because when dealing with green wood, the large teeth will prevent the saw from binding in the cut and will quickly carry the sawdust out. The longer the blade, the better, but look for anything with a folding blade 10–14 in. (25–35cm) long.

SHARPENING YOUR TOOLS

Often one of the biggest learning curves in getting started with woodworking is learning how to sharpen your tools. This is a skill in its own right, and takes practice. Fortunately there are many fantastic tutorial videos online that show the proper methods and movements of sharpening the specific tools that I have mentioned (see Resources on page 141). There are many opinions about the best sharpening methods, but in reality the best method is the one you use consistently.

For our purposes, there are really two sharpening methods you will find yourself leaning toward. The first uses a set of sticks with a radiused edge along one side that matches the inside curve of your hook knife,

with automotive sandpaper adhered and wrapped around it. I carry five in my own tool kit—the grits are as follows: 220, 400, 800, 1500, and then a leather-wrapped "strop" that is charged with honing compound. These will be used to keep your knives razor sharp, correcting the normal edge wear that happens during carving.

At some point you will have a major nick in your cutting edge from either dropping it on the ground or from accidentally bumping up against another metal tool. In order to correct this, you will need a coarse sharpening stone that can grind back the cutting edge and remove the nick. I recommend a coarse diamond stone or a water stone of 100–200 grit.

One of the biggest learning curves is sharpening and maintaining your tools to get the best and cleanest cuts.

SAFETY

The techniques used in this book have been in practice for hundreds of years. The grips and movements listed on the following pages are by no means comprehensive, but an awareness of basic principles will prevent the majority of injuries. Always take a second or two to ask: "Where can this knife/hatchet go?" When the knife leaves the wood, will your cut go into open air or could it hit your hand? Look at the full movement of your cut or hatchet swing. I will often stop to check if a leg could possibly be in the way if my hatchet misses the chopping block on the way down. If there is a chance it could, I adjust my stance to accommodate.

The other equally good question to ask is: "What will stop the knife/hatchet from hitting me?" Sometimes it could be that your range of motion is limited, as when you are using only your wrist for a cut with no arm strength behind it. Or it could be that your hands are positioned behind the piece you are working with.

Safety becomes a habit that will protect you from potentially serious injuries. It is while you are learning to carve that your habits are being formed for the future.

In any case, always, always be aware of where your body is in relation to the sharp tools you are using. Do this and you will be fine. I have only ever had one close call in the 1,000,000+ cuts I estimate I have made, and it was due to me not paying attention to these principles. See the publisher's note on page 2 for more guidance on woodworking safety.

SAFETY MATERIALS

You should always have a well-stocked first-aid kit on hand. The most common injuries are small nicks and scratches that come from working around sharp knives and rough wood. Take extra precaution in starting out slowly and carefully building your muscle memory and familiarity with your tools through hard-won practice. As the old adage says: "Slow becomes steady and steady becomes fast." One small safety device I use on a regular basis is a wide, thick piece of leather to brace against my chest when carving toward myself.

Always be aware of where your body is in relation to the sharp tools you are using.

KNIFE WORK

A knife is an ancient tool that has been used in artisan work for thousands of years. A familiar and sharp knife quickly becomes an indispensable tool. It is capable of wasting away large strips of wood when backed by powerful strokes, or shaving away a whisper of wood fiber when used with a delicate hand. When you become skilled with a knife, you will have acquired some know-how that will never leave you. The following techniques will provide the foundations of that expertise.

Power cuts use the full strength of your arm.

HOW TO HOLD A KNIFE

The most important thing when holding a knife is a firm grip that allows you control. Often the way you are holding a knife is dictated by the kind of cut you are performing. At its most basic, your neutral grip should be similar to how you grasp a doorknob or when turning a car key in the ignition.

POWER CUT

This cut uses the full strength of your arm to quickly waste away wood in long powerful strokes. Start by grasping the knife in your hand with the cutting edge facing away from you. Slightly angle the tip of the knife upward while locking your wrist and elbow. Hold the wood firmly and to the side of your leg, bracing the piece against your body. With a straight arm, and with the power coming from your shoulder, push the cutting edge downward and all the way to the end of your cut. The knife should cut down away from you and into the open air.

CHEST-LEVER CUT

This is another powerful cut, utilizing the leverage from your back muscles. The movement here is very similar to using a giant pair of scissors. With your palm up, grasp the knife in your cutting hand, bevel edge facing away from you. In your other hand, grasp the workpiece the same way.

You will cut with the knife starting close to the handle and moving toward the tip as the cut moves through the wood. Your forearms should roll against your torso and end with your elbows. Done right, this technique will create long, strong cuts.

Chest-lever cuts utilize leverage from your back muscles and create long, strong cuts.

Cut with the knife starting close to the handle and moving toward the tip.

The knife should stay at the same angle, tip pointed away and handle facing you.

PULL CUT

Also known as a pull stroke or a planing cut, this is the cut that I rely on the most. Pinch the back of the blade right above the handle between your thumb and index finger. Hold with the tip of the knife pointed away from you, lock your wrist, and pull the knife down the cut by pulling your elbow back along your rib cage. The knife should stay at the same angle, tip pointed away and handle facing you. There should be no wrist movement in the cut. Your wrist and forearm will act as a natural stop for the knife. This enables long and powerful strokes as well as allowing you to take smooth shavings during finishing. Common knife wisdom would say that you should never cut toward yourself. If done the right way, however, it becomes safe and very effective.

THUMB-LEVER CUT

This cut is used for taking fine shavings to shape surfaces, such as the back of spoon bowls or the edges and ends of a workpiece. This is another go-to cut I find myself using often. Starting from a standard grip, turn your wrist over so that the cutting edge faces away from you with your fingers pointed down. The thumb of your knife hand should be on the back of the blade, just above the handle. Your opposite hand will simultaneously support the work and act as the fulcrum for the knife. This thumb will remain stationary, employing only a light push; while your other hand rolls, the back of the knife hinges on your thumb.

The thumb of your knife hand should be at the back of the blade, just above the handle.

SCOOP CUT

If you have ever seen someone peel a potato with a knife, this is the grip they are using. Hold the knife with a standard knife grip, rotating your hand so that the blade points toward your thumb. Wrap your thumb around the workpiece. You will then open and close your hand using the remaining four fingers, squeezing your hand into the open air between your thumb and forefinger. Make sure your thumb is well below the area of cut. Also known as a paring cut, you can practice this cut by peeling a potato or an apple with a kitchen paring knife, as this will train you in the correct movement. The most important thing is to make sure your thumb is not in the way.

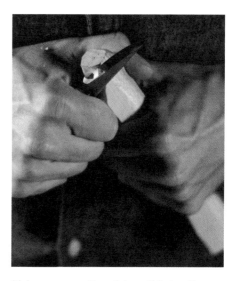

Make sure your thumb is well below the area of the cut.

PREPARING A BLANK

A "blank" refers to a piece of wood cut down from a larger piece of wood or log. Every project will require that you start with a piece of wood of a specific thickness, width, and length. I will quickly go through the process of preparing a blank for your first project.

1 Start with a freshly cut branch or piece of trunk, approximately 3–8 in. (7.5–20cm) in diameter. Split it in half using either a wedge and sledgehammer or a splitting axe. Most pieces of green wood will split right down the middle, but you may encounter a twisted piece that splits with "webs" or wood fibers that cross both sides. If this happens, carefully cut away with a hatchet.

2 Take one of the split pieces and split it in half again. You now have a quarter log. As you begin to work with your hatchet at the chopping block, take care to never work more than two-thirds of the way up the blank, guarding your fingers by supporting the piece from behind the wood. Your hatchet cuts should be consistent and unchanged, moving 90 degrees or the natural arc of your elbow with your wrist locked. You will achieve different cuts by slightly raising and lowering the blank as you cut.

3 At the chopping block, remove the pith from the middle of the tree by taking a series of relief cuts up the length, chopping into the pith with the blank lowered and then taking longer cuts by raising it slightly. Flip the blank over and repeat the process.

4 Remove the bark in the same manner, then square up the blank by removing the shorter angled side down the length of the wood.

5 You should be left with a roughly rectangular length of wood with no bark that is ready to be used for a new project.

FINISHING

It is important to properly finish your whittled projects, not only to improve their final appearance but also to protect the completed item when it is being put to use. The best finishing techniques to use depends on the item that you are creating. Finishing guidance is provided for each project in the book, but some common methods are described below.

SANDING

It is quite possible to become skilled enough with your knives that you can create smooth, flat surfaces with knives alone. However, it is often the case that you will need sandpaper to smooth out and correct irregular lines and bumps, particularly in your first woodworking projects.

Sandpaper works by removing wood fibers using abrasives of various particle size stuck to paper. These particles are commonly referred to as the "grit." The larger the particle size, the faster the wood will wear away and the coarser the surface left behind. Each increase in grit removes the scratches left by the previous grit size. The key to flawless surfaces is patiently working up through the grits. The grit size of sandpaper is usually given as a number inversely related to the particle size. For example, start with 80 and then move on to 120, 180, 220, 400, and finally 600.

The main mistake that people make when using sandpaper is unintentionally rounding over the edges of their work. This makes facets and bevels look sloppy, and is the result of not being aware of how your fingers are folding the paper over the edges on your workpiece. Paying attention to this will result in clean, crisp, even surfaces.

Sanding is great for smoothing out and correcting your first carving projects.

KNIFE FINISH

A "knife finish" is the surface left on a workpiece by a well-sharpened knife. Usually smooth and richly textured, it is often a surface that does not need to be cleaned up by sanding. A knife can shear wood fibers to leave a smooth surface unrivaled by other methods. A knife finish will retain its effect even under repeated washings and will create jewel-like facets on the backs of bowls and long, smooth, textured surfaces on handles.

OILS

For items that will be used in the kitchen, the best oils to use for finishing your projects are often the same ones used for cooking. My favorite oils are flaxseed oil and walnut oil. Man-made oils such as mineral oil are also fine to use, as they do not dry and will wash away in the sink. It is a good rule of thumb to only use "food-safe" oils on anything that will touch food. For everything else decorative, use furniture-grade finishes such as tung oil or wipe-on polyurethanes—anything that will give you a "rubbed" finish; not too shiny, but showcasing the texture of the wood.

Only use food-safe oils on items that will come into contact with anything edible.

PROJECTS

BUTTER PADDLE

MATERIALS
- Freshly split log 4–6 in. (10–15cm) across by 10 in. (25cm) long, or a dry softwood board approx. ½ x 2 x 10 in. (1.3 x 5 x 25cm); dogwood was used here
- Hatchet (if using log)
- Pen or pencil
- Straight knife
- Saw
- Sandpaper
- Oil

A butter paddle is something you may not already have in your kitchen, but once you do, you will wonder how you ever lived without one. This simple project will exercise all of your knife skills.

BASIC SHAPE

1 If you are starting with a log, use a hatchet to split out a thin board, roughly ½ in. (1.3cm) thick. Pay attention to the direction of the grain, because you need a radially cut board.

2 Draw the shape of the butter paddle onto the wood, taking care to align the length of the paddle with the grain.

3 Using a straight knife and long power cuts, begin carving away the wood along the length of the paddle. This will establish the profile of the sides. Leave the top and bottom intact to allow for better grip.

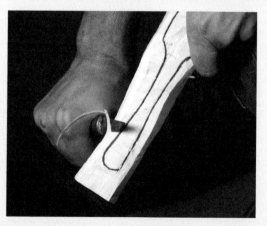

4 Saw off any excess wood from the ends of the paddle.

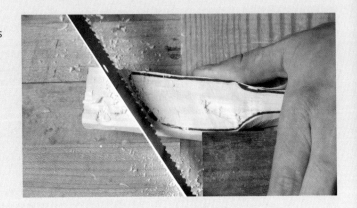

BEVELS

5 Mark out the bevels around the handle. This is also a good time to mark a centerline all around the sides of the paddle (visible in step 7). You may need to redraw the centerline as you carve, but it will help you to keep things symmetrical. Working with the grain, start carving the bevels on each side of the handle. Use pull cuts to work down each marked slope from both ends, so that the cuts meet in the middle.

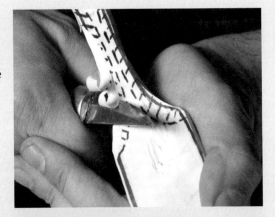

6 Round off the end of the handle, working to the outline using thumb-lever cuts. This will make it more comfortable as you begin to use pull cuts to shape the bevel around the end of the handle.

7 Mark the wider bevels on the blade of the paddle. You may find that you need to redraw the centerline around the sides. Start to carve the wider bevels using a very shallow angle of cut. Take care not to split the wood, because you are working along the grain. Use a slicing cut to keep the edge clean.

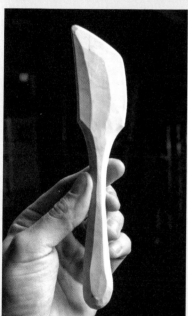

8 Now begin adding some detail. Start by carving in the three-dimensionality of the curves, trying to make the sides of the paddle even. A slight bevel along the top edge of the blade will reduce the visual weight of the piece. Next, smooth out the bevels by taking finer, smaller cuts.

FINISHING

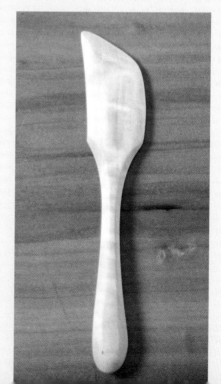

9 Once you are happy with the shape, sand everything smooth, but take care not to erase the definition of your carving. Oil as desired.

SPATULA

Arguably the most important tool in the kitchen, a spatula is a cooking workhorse. This example can be tailored to your cooking style, hand, and pot. A similar shape to the butter paddle, it will allow you to refine your techniques.

MATERIALS
- 3 x 14 in. (7.5 x 36cm) piece of wood, about ¾–1 in. (2–2.5cm) thick; cherry was used here
- Pen or pencil
- Saw
- Hatchet
- Straight knife
- Sandpaper (optional)
- Oil

BASIC SHAPE

1 Draw the shape of the spatula onto the wood, with a centerline running down the length of the handle. I divided the length of the spatula into four equal parts, and made the head one part and the handle three parts.

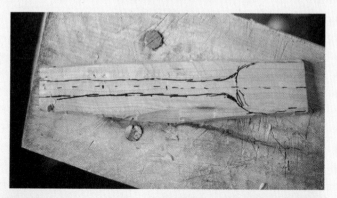

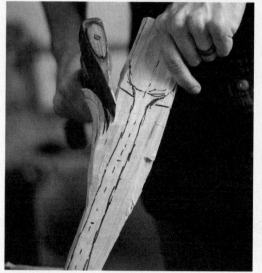

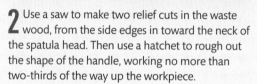

2 Use a saw to make two relief cuts in the waste wood, from the side edges in toward the neck of the spatula head. Then use a hatchet to rough out the shape of the handle, working no more than two-thirds of the way up the workpiece.

3 Carefully chop out the wood as far as the sawn relief cuts, taking care around the neck where the handle meets the head.

4 Smooth the transition at the neck by taking very light chops, making sure you support the workpiece as you do so.

5 Draw the side profile of the spatula onto the wood, then use the hatchet to even out the thickness of the front and back.

REFINING THE SHAPE

6 Switch to a straight knife and use long power cuts to begin refining the shape of the handle.

7 Just below the neck of the spatula, use pull cuts to carve the handle, moving toward the head and stopping at the place where the grain changes.

8 Now work down the slope from the head of the spatula to the handle to smooth the curve of the neck.

9 Use pushing thumb-lever cuts to flatten and smooth the front and back faces of the spatula head.

10 Begin to straighten the lines of the handle. Look for any high or low spots as you slide down the length of the spatula, making sure you are carving straight lines.

11 If you started with green wood, allow the workpiece to dry overnight. Then use a freshly sharpened knife to refine the overall shape of the spatula. Smooth any rough cuts with the knife, connecting all the lines so that all faces meld smoothly into each other.

FINISHING

12 Shape the end of the spatula handle and remove any hard edges from the handle and head. I have also carved a small notch at the upper corner of the head. Leave the spatula knife-finished or sand all surfaces smooth. Oil as desired.

SERVING BOARD

A serving board is a good thing to have on hand when entertaining guests. It can be used to display food or serve drinks. Once you have followed the process here, you will be able to make a serving board of any shape and size to suit your purpose.

MATERIALS

- ¾ x 6 x 20 in. (2 x 15 x 50cm) piece of wood; poplar was used here
- Rule and/or dividers
- Pen or pencil
- Saw
- Clamp
- Hatchet
- Mallet
- Straight knife
- Drill and ⅜ in. (10mm) bit
- Sandpaper
- Oil

BASIC SHAPE

1 Decide on the dimensions of your serving board. I decided to make the overall length three times the width of the board, with the handle being 6 in. (15cm) long and the serving area 12 in. (30cm) long.

2 Mark a centerline running down the length of the board. This will help you to keep the serving board symmetrical. Draw the curves of the handle and the placement of the hanging hole.

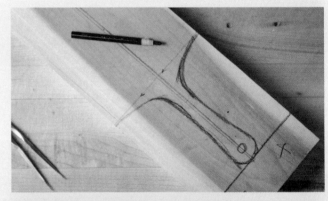

3 Use a saw to make two relief cuts in the waste wood around the handle, from the side edges in toward the base of the handle where it meets the main board.

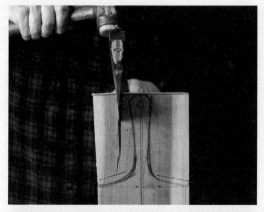

4 Clamp the board upright on your worktable. Using a hatchet with a mallet to control the force, split away half of the wood between the edge of the board and the side of the handle. Watch the grain of the wood to make sure that the split does not run into the handle. Repeat on the other side.

5 With the board properly braced, use the hatchet on its own to take small cuts and work closer to the lines of the handle. Work no more than two-thirds of the way up the handle.

6 Switch to a straight knife and carve down to the lines of the handle, paying attention to the direction of the grain.

BEVELS

7 With the profile
established, mark
guidelines for the bevels
all around the board
and handle, about ¼ in.
(5mm) in from the edge.

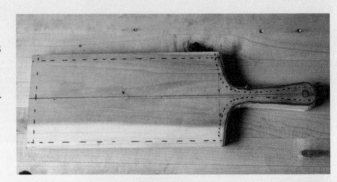

8 Use the straight knife to shave away
wood for the bevels, working down
to the guidelines. Start with the sides,
then move on to the end of the board,
and finally the handle.

9 If you wish, you can blend the bevel
into slightly curved sides by adding
a bit of interesting texture. Do this by
carving carefully and consistently
along the edges.

FINISHING

10 With the sides completed, brace the piece and carefully drill the hanging hole, making sure to back the workpiece with scrap wood where the drill exits so as not to split the wood.

11 Sand the board clean on the top and bottom, but leave the sides unsanded to keep the texture intact. Be sure not to round off the edges of the board. Oil as desired.

COOKING SPOON

A well-made cooking spoon will be part of a kitchen for decades. Built on the foundations of the butter paddle and spatula, this project will also give you practice in using a hook knife to make bowls and concave surfaces, which are key to spoons.

BASIC SHAPE

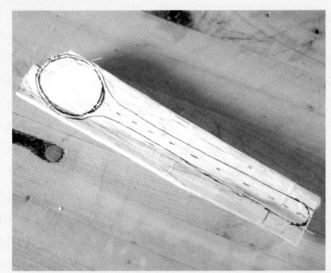

1 Draw the shape of the spoon onto the wood, with a centerline running down the length of the handle. I divided the length of the spoon into four equal parts, and made the bowl one part and the handle three parts.

2 Using the same technique as for the spatula (steps 2–5, pages 35–36), saw two relief cuts just below the neck of the bowl and then use a hatchet to cut down to the rough profile lines.

3 Sketch the side profile of the spoon onto the side of the wood, then carve down to the drawn lines with the hatchet.

4 Switch to a straight knife and clean up the profile by carving down to the outline. Begin to give the handle shape, using planing pull cuts down the length of the handle to make it straight and smooth.

BOWL

5 Use the straight knife and thumb-lever cuts to give the back of the bowl its shape.

6 Switch to a hook knife and use scoop cuts to carve the inside of the bowl. Paying attention to the direction of the grain, begin by taking shavings across the grain, working from the sides toward the middle of the bowl.

7 Once the shape of the bowl has been established, make very light cuts to smooth the inside and even out the shape.

8 If you are working with green wood, set the spoon aside to dry for about a day. Then resharpen the straight knife and start to refine the overall shape of the spoon, smoothing transitions and any rough or uneven spots.

FINISHING

9 Leave the spoon knife-finished or sand all surfaces smooth. Oil as desired.

MATERIALS

- Freshly split quarter log
  4–5 in. (10–12.5cm) thick,
  6–7 in. (15–18cm) at widest point,
  and 12–14 in. (30–36cm) long;
  cherry was used here
- Hatchet
- Saw (optional)
- Pen or pencil
- Rule and/or dividers
- Compass
- Hook knife
- Drill and 7/8 in. (20mm) bit (adjust
  size of bit to suit your candles)
- Straight knife
- Sandpaper
- Oil

CANDLEHOLDER

This is a fun project, albeit a little challenging. I have used the grain of the wood and the texture created by the hook knife to carve a candleholder reminiscent of the landscape of the American Southwest.

BASIC SHAPE

1 Start with a freshly cut quarter of a log. You will be carving the "landscape" from the bark side toward the heart of the tree.

2 On the side opposite the bark, use a hatchet or saw to remove the pith and create a large flat surface. This will form the bottom of the candleholder.

3 Use the hatchet to remove the bark and start to carve away the sides. Take care to leave the mass down the center of the length of wood to form the highpoints of the landscape.

4 Draw a centerline down the length of the wood and divide it into four equal sections. The dividing marks indicate where the three "mountains" will be carved as candleholders.

5 Use a compass to draw a 1 in. (2.5cm) diameter circle for each candle hole, with a wider 2 in. (5cm) diameter circle around them to mark the outer circumference of the mountaintops. Mark the wood around the outer circles to indicate where you will carve the texture of the landscape.

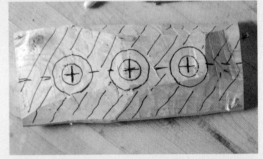

6 Use a hook knife to begin carving the mountainsides and the canyon walls. Right now you are just removing the mass before moving on to sculpting. Take care to leave a solid thickness for the base.

DRILLING AND REFINING

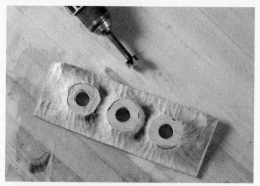

7 Once you have carved up to the edges of the larger circles and the general shape has been established, you can drill the holes for the candles. Check the size of your candles to determine the size of the holes. I used 1 in. (2.5cm) thick candles that tapered down to ⅞ in. (2cm), so I drilled ⅞ in. (2cm) diameter holes.

8 Continue to refine the shape with the hook knife, carving close to the edges of the holes. Lighter cuts will increase the texture. Try to remove any nicks or deep gouges, smoothing all of the lines into one another. Clean the top surfaces with a straight knife, removing any pen or pencil marks as you do so.

FINISHING

9 Use a very high-grit sandpaper to lightly sand the whole piece, following the lines of the cuts. Oil as desired.

SALT CELLAR

If you get into cooking, chances are you will want a place to keep your salt close by. A salt cellar keeps this most important seasoning on hand in a fancy, protected way.

MATERIALS
- 4 x 4 x 4 in. (10 x 10 x 10cm) piece of wood; ambrosia maple was used here
- Pen or pencil
- Compass
- Saw
- Hook knife
- Straight knife
- Sandpaper
- Oil

BOWL

1 Draw a 3 in. (7.5cm) diameter circle in the center of the wood.

2 Use a saw to remove as much of the excess wood from around the circle as possible.

3 Use the saw to slice about a third off the top. The thicker piece will be the bowl of the cellar and the thinner slice will form the lid. Redraw the circle onto the thicker piece.

4 Start to hollow out the bowl of the cellar using a hook knife. Carve across the grain using scoop cuts, working from the sides toward the middle of the bowl.

5 Continue hollowing out the bowl, making sure to stop approximately ¼ in. (5mm) in from the edge. Once the shape has been established, take very light cuts to smooth the inside and even out the bowl.

6 Switch to a straight knife and use scoop cuts to round off the outside walls of the cellar bowl. I chose to make this cellar straight-walled from top to bottom, but you can carve the outside into a rounded bowl shape if you prefer.

7 Use the straight knife to carve the profile of the lid down to the drawn outline. At this point, both the lid and bowl should be circular and equal in size.

8 The lid can be as simple as a flat circle or you can add a small handle. Start by marking off a strip across the center for the handle, and draw a guideline around the edge of the lid to indicate how deep the handle will be. Use the hook knife to carve away the wood on either side of the handle, working across the grain away from the center on either side until you have a rough raised handle.

9 Once you are happy with the shape of the lid and handle, switch to the straight knife to smooth and straighten the surface.

10 Use the straight knife to carve the outside of the lid slightly undersized. Place the lid onto the cellar bowl and draw around it to transfer the shape of the lid onto the bowl.

11 Carve the inside of the bowl up to the line you transferred from the lid, using the hook knife to smooth and even out the bowl surface.

FINISHING

12 Use the straight knife to carve a small bevel on the underside edge of the lid to allow it to seat in the bowl. Allow to it dry if you have used freshly cut wood, then lightly sand. Oil as desired.

DOORSTOP

Doorstops are a simple wedge shape, which makes this the perfect project for when you are looking for something quick and easy to carve. It also provides an elegant and practical solution to a common and simple problem.

MATERIALS

- 1½ x 1½ x 5 in. (4 x 4 x 12.5cm) piece of wood; black walnut was used here
- Pen or pencil
- Hatchet
- Hook knife and/or straight knife
- Sandpaper
- Oil

SHAPING

1 Draw the outline of the doorstop onto the side profile of the wood and mark the waste wood that needs to be removed.

2 Use a hatchet to remove the waste from the long slope of the doorstop. Make careful and controlled cuts, and be sure to guard your fingers behind the workpiece. Next, use the hatchet to rough out the back of the stop.

3 Use a knife to refine the shape of the doorstop. The slope on this example has a bit of a curve to it, so I found it easier to use a hook knife, but a straight knife would work easily too.

4 Continue to refine the shape, taking care to reserve a wide flat area at the tapered end.

5 Use the knife to round off the back of the doorstop. This will give it a faceted knife-finished look. I carved a decorative taper at the end of the doorstop using a straight knife (visible in step 6).

FINISHING

6 Using high-grit sandpaper (600 or above), sand the doorstop smooth or leave the facets visible. Oil as desired.

SPICE SPOON

A spice spoon is a long-handled spoon that can fit into the small opening of a spice jar. They are quick and easy to make, and with a single wedge of wood you can make enough spoons for your kitchen to always have one on hand.

MATERIALS

- Approx. ½ x 1 x 10 in. (1.3 x 2.5 x 25cm) piece of wood per spoon; cherry was used here
- Pen or pencil
- Saw
- Straight knife
- Hook knife
- Sandpaper
- Oil

BASIC SHAPE

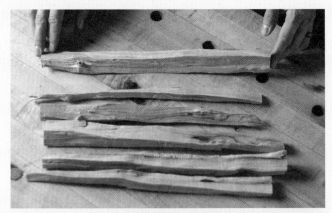

1 Decide how long you would like the spoon to be. Long ones are nice and you can hold several in a small jar on the kitchen counter. I have used a piece of wood split into sections to make several spoons, each roughly 9 in. (23cm) long.

2 Draw the shape of the spoon onto the wood, with a centerline running down the length of the handle. I divided the length of the spoon into seven equal parts, and made the head one part and the handle six parts plus an extra half.

3 Use a saw to cut off any waste wood from the ends.

HANDLE AND BOWL

4 Use a straight knife to carve away some of the wood from the sides. Don't carve right up to the lines yet—the spoon has a very thin handle, so you need to leave some wood to hold onto while carving the bowl.

5 Use a hook knife to carve out the bowl, making careful and safe cuts. The bowl of this spoon is about ½ in. (1.3cm) at its widest point, but the width is really determined by the spice jars in your kitchen. When you have finished the bowl, use the straight knife to carve away the wood around the edges.

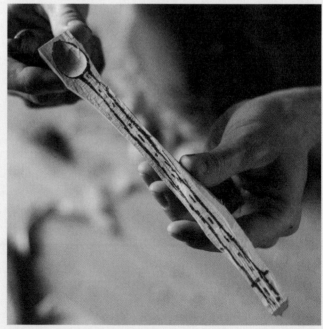

6 Using the straight knife and very careful pull cuts, begin to thin down the handle. Take care not to apply too much pressure, because the handle is fragile and may break as it is thinned out.

7 Using the straight knife and a thumb-lever grip, gently carve the outside of the bowl using very small cuts. Take care because it is easy to break the spoon at this point if too much pressure is used.

FINISHING

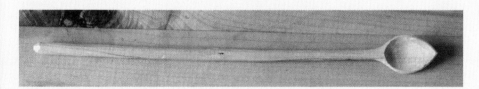

8 If you started with green wood, let the wood dry overnight. Then resharpen the straight knife and refine the shape, taking very light shavings to smooth the overall piece. Sand the spoon and oil as desired.

FORK

You could create your own charming dinnerware set by carving a spoon, butter knife, and fork. A fork is more of a challenge than the others, but a challenge usually ends with a reward. Take special care to follow the grain of the wood, so as not to create weak tines that can easily break.

MATERIALS

- ½ x 1 x 12 in. (1.3 x 2.5 x 30cm) piece of wood; cherry was used here
- Pen or pencil
- Thin-bladed saw
- Straight knife
- Hook knife
- Sandpaper
- Oil

BASIC SHAPE

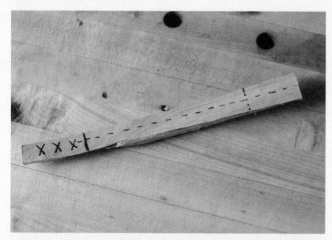

1 Choose a piece of wood where the grain runs along its length, so that the tines of the fork can follow it for strength. Draw a centerline down the face of the wood and divide the length into four equal sections; the head will be one part, and the handle about two-and-a-half parts. Saw off any waste wood.

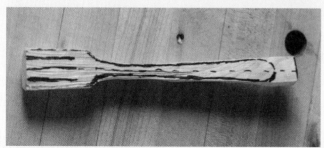

2 Draw the shape of the fork onto the wood. Use a straight knife to carve away the sides of the handle down to the outline.

3 Draw the side profile of the fork onto the wood, making sure that the tines of the fork follow the grain as closely as possible. Use the straight knife to carve the handle down to the drawn lines of the side profile.

4 Now move on to the head of the fork. It helps to think of this as a very shallow spoon. Use a hook knife to carve the inside of the "bowl" and the straight knife to round the back of it. Redraw the four tines onto the front.

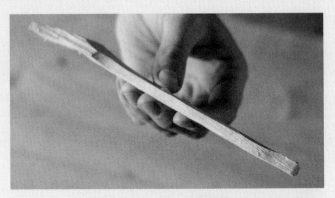

5 Use the straight knife and pull cuts to give shape to the handle. Aim for symmetry on both sides of the handle. If you would like to add a decorative element to the end of the handle, now is the time. I chose to carve a point (visible in step 8).

TINES

6 Using a thin-bladed saw, very carefully cut three equal grooves into the head of the fork to separate the tines. It will be fragile, so take care to support the back of the fork while you saw.

7 Paying attention to the direction of the grain and with great care, use the straight knife to begin carving a bevel along the edges of each tine.

8 Work systematically, carving all the right-side edges and then all the left-side edges. Turn the fork over and repeat on the back. Continue to carve these bevels until they meet each other and the grooves start to open up. Finish by carving a point on each tine.

FINISHING

9 Starting with low-grit sandpaper (try 150), sand the inside of the tines, sliding the sandpaper in between the grooves until everything is smoothed out. Sand the rest of the fork, then oil as desired.

LADLE

MATERIALS
- Large and long piece of wood; a split cherry log about 3 x 4 x 16 in. (7.5 x 10 x 40cm) was used here
- Pen or pencil
- Hatchet
- Saw
- Straight knife
- Hook knife
- Sandpaper
- Oil

Ladles are the time-honored way of serving soups and stews from deep pots and bowls. The best wood for a ladle is the crook of a tree branch, but one can also be made with a straight piece, as shown here.

BASIC SHAPE

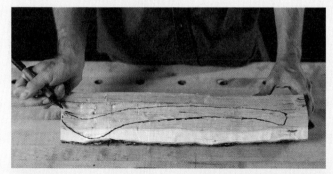

1 Draw the side profile of the ladle onto the wood, paying attention to the orientation of the grain so that it runs along the length of the ladle. Use a hatchet to remove wood down to the drawn lines.

2 Draw a centerline down the top face of the wood and use it to help you draw the top profile of the ladle symmetrically.

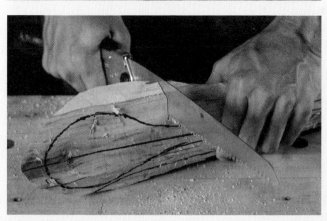

3 Using the same technique as for the spatula (steps 2–5, pages 35–36), saw two relief cuts near the neck of the ladle, and then work down to the lines with the hatchet.

4 Draw the side profile onto the wood and then carve down to the lines using the hatchet.

HANDLE AND BOWL

5 With the top and side profiles established, switch to a straight knife to shape the handle. Use long pull cuts to clean up the form by knocking off the corners and making everything somewhat smooth. Work down to the lines, noting that you are not doing finishing cuts but just enough to get to the next step.

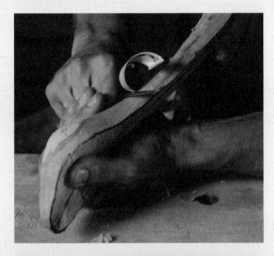

6 Mark where the bowl will be hollowed out. This will prevent you from carving too near to the edge and will show you how much wood has been removed as you progress.

7 Switch to a hook knife to carve the bowl, working across the grain toward the middle from both sides. This will take some time because the bowl of a ladle is quite deep.

8 Flip the ladle over and smooth the underside of the bowl using the straight knife and pushing thumb-lever cuts. Resharpen the knife and begin the finishing cuts, smoothing out any surfaces and connecting any lines on the handle and bowl.

FINISHING

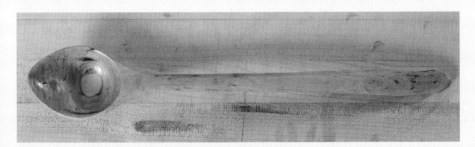

9 If you started with green wood, allow the ladle to dry overnight before sanding the bowl and handle smooth. Oil as desired.

MATERIALS

- 1 x 3 x 12 in. (2.5 x 7.5 x 30cm) piece of wood; black walnut was used here
- Pen or pencil
- Saw
- Hatchet
- Mallet
- Straight knife
- Hook knife
- Drill and 3/16 in. (5mm) bit
- Sandpaper
- Oil

SLOTTED SPOON

An often reached for tool in the kitchen is the trusty slotted spoon. Made to strain and sieve, this spoon is a tool easily made with the skills gained from carving the cooking spoon.

BASIC SHAPE

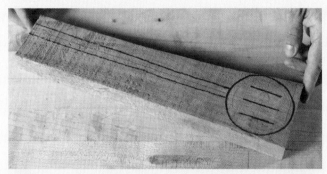

1 Draw the outline of the spoon onto the top face of the wood and roughly mark where the slots should go.

2 Use a saw to carefully make two relief cuts into the neck where the handle meets the bowl of the spoon.

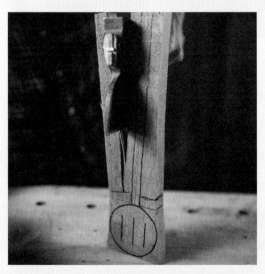

3 Use a hatchet and mallet to split out the waste around the handle.

4 Work down to the lines on both the handle and the bowl using the hatchet.

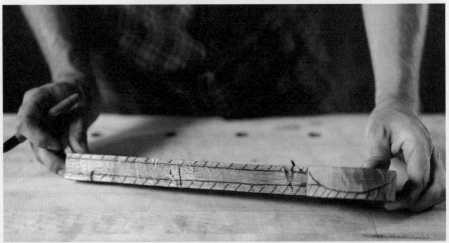

5 With the top profile established, draw the side profile onto the wood. Use the hatchet to work down to the lines, and then use a straight knife to straighten and smooth the handle.

BOWL AND SLOTS

6 Use a hook knife to hollow out the inside of the bowl. If you are using seasoned wood like me, this process will take longer.

7 Once the inside is hollowed out, use the straight knife to shape the curve of the back of the bowl.

8 Use the straight knife to clean up the neck of the handle where it meets the bowl and give it more definition.

9 With the spoon almost complete, redraw the lines for the slots. Use a drill to make a series of holes along the lines of each slot. I drilled four holes per slot.

10 Using the straight knife, carve a V-shaped groove along each line from the inside of the bowl. Flip the spoon over and repeat this process from the outside of the bowl, until the grooves become slots. With your knife, flatten and clear out the holes as best as you can.

FINISHING

11 Starting with low-grit sandpaper, sand everything smooth. Fold the sandpaper to sand the insides of the slots until smooth. Oil as desired.

TOOL HANDLE

If you use tools such as a knife, hatchet, or hammer, at some point the handle will become worn and damaged and will eventually need to be replaced. Using your skill as a carver, you can quickly and easily restore these tools while also adding a personalized look.

MATERIALS
- 1 x 1 x 10 in. (2.5 x 2.5 x 25cm) piece of wood, or size to suit the handle you are replacing; black walnut was used here
- Pen and pencil
- Straight knife
- Sandpaper
- Saw
- Drill and ³⁄₁₆ in. (5mm) bit
- Scrap of wood to make wedge
- Glue
- Mallet
- Oil

BASIC SHAPE

1 The wood should be the thickness of the hammerhead or taken from the size of the eye, plus ¼ in. (5mm) all around. If you have the original handle for your tool, measure that. Draw the shape of the handle onto the side of the wood.

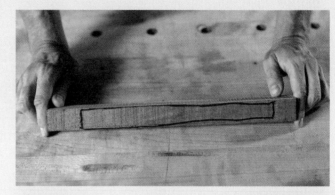

2 Use a straight knife to remove wood down to the drawn outline. Begin to smooth and straighten the handle, taking care to leave the end that gets inserted into the hammerhead slightly larger than the opening.

3 Hold the hammerhead in place on top of the handle and use a long pencil to trace the opening onto the end of the wood.

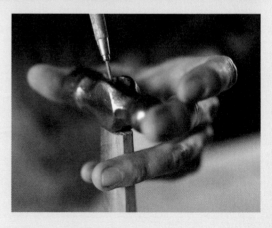

4 Carefully carve down to the traced outline with the knife.

5 Use a pencil to spread graphite around the inside of the opening on the hammerhead. This will reveal any tight spots and allow you to sneak up on the right fit.

6 Insert the handle into the opening until it becomes tight, but not so tight that it cannot be removed by hand. When you remove the handle, you will see graphite marks left behind from the spots that are too tight a fit.

7 Very carefully and lightly shave these spots away with the knife. Repeat the process of test fitting and adjusting until the hammerhead fits snugly onto the handle.

8 Once you are certain of the fit, take a moment to finesse any details on the handle. Sand it smooth, but leave the part that is inserted into the head untouched.

ASSEMBLY

9 Use a saw to cut down the center of part that will be fitted into the hammerhead, then drill a hole at the bottom of the cut. This will relieve the splitting pressure exerted by the wedge that will be inserted next.

10 Attach the hammerhead to the handle and prepare a wedge of wood as wide as the hammerhead opening. Glue one side only of the wedge and then drive the wedge into the cut in the tool handle with a mallet. It should finish flush with the handle, so trim the end if necessary.

FINISHING

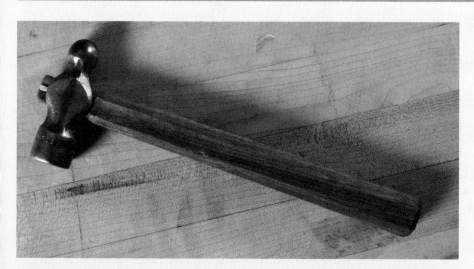

11 Allow the glue to dry and then oil as desired.

Making your own tool
handle lets you create
a bespoke tool to your
own requirements.

MOBILE

Mobiles are a great way to add a point of interest to your decor—a bit of visual magic and movement. This project will help you to create a one-of-a-kind piece and put your carving skills on display.

MATERIALS

- Two 3 x 10 in. (7.5 x 25cm) pieces of different types of wood, each about 1½–2 in. (4–5cm) thick; cherry and sycamore were used here
- Hatchet
- Straight knife
- Saw
- Metallic wax
- Cloth
- Drill and small drill bit
- Nylon thread or fishing line
- Sewing needle (optional)
- Three lengths of dowel, one about 20 in. (50cm) long and two about 10 in. (25cm) long

FACETED SHAPES

1 This is a good project for combining different types of wood; try using woods that are different colors. Although I have used two long pieces, you can use any small interesting offcuts. Mark out five different-sized shapes onto the wood.

2 Starting with the shape nearest the end of the wood, use a hatchet to roughly define the piece.

3 If the end piece is small, you may find it easier to carve the facets while it is still attached to the length of wood. Use a straight knife to clean up the roughness and smooth the surfaces, and then carve jewel-like facets into the piece.

4 Use a saw to cut the piece from the length of wood when your have finished shaping it.

5 For a larger piece, you can cut the roughly shaped piece off the length of wood and hold it in your hand as you refine its shape.

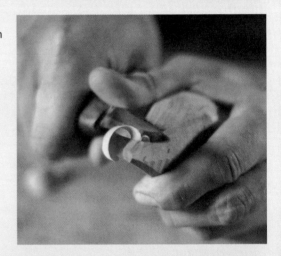

6 The larger and longer cuts you take, the smoother the carved facets of the piece will be.

7 Once you have carved all five shapes, you may wish to embellish a few (or all) of them with metallic wax. You can buy metallic wax at most craft stores. Simply rub the wax onto the wood and then buff to a sheen with a cloth.

ASSEMBLY

8 Use a small-diameter bit to drill a hole across the topmost part of each piece for the thread to go through.

9 Thread a length of nylon thread or fishing line through the hole on each piece. Use a sewing needle as an aide if you have trouble fitting the thread through the hole. Tie with a secure knot and leave a generous length of thread for hanging.

10 Arrange the mobile pieces and then assemble from the bottom up. Begin by tying two pieces onto each of the shorter dowels, one at each end. Next, tie another piece to the center of the longer dowel.

11 Balancing the mobile will take some trial and error. You can quickly find the balancing point on each of the smaller dowels by balancing the dowel on your finger. This is the point where you will hang it from the topmost dowel.

12 Tie the two shorter dowels to the longer top one, shifting each of the smaller dowels right and left until the mobile is balanced. Tie a length of thread to the top dowel for hanging the mobile.

CARVED ANIMAL

Carved animals are probably the most traditional and classic whittled design, and every culture has its own variation. They will challenge your carving ability by forcing you to think about three-dimensional forms. The goal here is not to be perfect, but rather to simplify a complex animal form into a recognizable shape. Aside from that, they make great gifts.

MATERIALS

- 1½ in. (4cm) thick piece of wood, at least 2 in. (5cm) wide by 10 in. (25cm) long; sycamore was used here
- Hatchet
- Saw
- Hook knife
- Straight knife
- Sandpaper (optional)
- Oil

BASIC SHAPE

1 Roughly draw the side profile of the animal you wish to carve onto the wood. Search the internet if you are unsure, looking for images of the animal from above and the side. I drew a hedgehog and a fox onto my piece of wood, so chop or saw them into separate pieces if you have also drawn more than one.

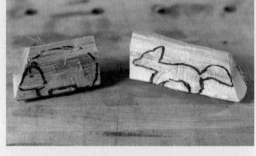

2 Begin to carve out the side profile. Start by using a hatchet to remove larger pieces of waste wood, taking small short chops with your hands safely guarded. Use a saw to make relief cuts where necessary, such as behind the fox's ears.

3 Use a hook knife to carve away the undersides and a straight knife to carve along the top, working down to the drawn lines.

DEFINITION

4 With the side profile established, use the straight knife to give the animal a more rounded shape. Remove the corners and create a taper from the midpoint of the body up to the top on both sides.

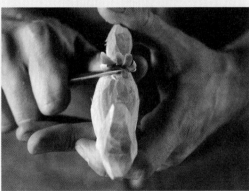

5 Round off the back of the animal, giving some definition to the head and the tail.

FINISHING

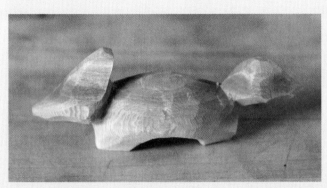

6 Correct any cut marks, then sand smooth if desired or leave the animal knife-finished. Oil as desired.

BOOKENDS

These bookends serve two purposes: form and function. Showing the natural patterns in the wood, these two endcaps become a statement piece for your bookshelves and will keep everything upright and neat.

MATERIALS

- Full log about 6–8 in. (15–20cm) diameter and 12–14 in. (30–36cm) long; cherry was used here
- Hatchet
- Saw
- Pen or pencil
- Straight knife
- Hook knife
- Sandpaper
- Oil or polyurethane

BASIC SHAPE

1 Bookends need to be heavy, so in order to achieve the required mass, start with a full log. Use a hatchet to split the log roughly in half and choose the thicker of the two pieces. Remove the pith and flatten the underside of the log with the hatchet.

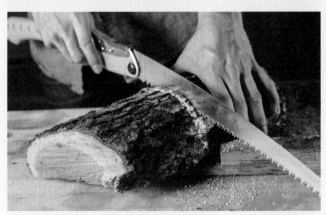

2 Saw the piece in half, one for each bookend. Because the bookends are carved from a freshly cut log and the pieces are so thick, cracking or "checking" will occur. This will add visual interest to the bookends and will not affect their function in any way.

3 Use the hatchet to remove the bark and smooth the outside of each cut piece.

4 Draw a curve from the bottom outside edge to the top inside edge on both pieces. Mark the waste wood on the outside of the curve.

5 Use the hatchet to carve away the waste wood, working down to the line and taking care to keep your hands behind the workpiece while keeping the piece properly supported.

REFINING AND TEXTURING

6 Starting with the hatchet and finishing with a straight knife, flatten the vertical side of each bookend—the side that will butt up against the books.

7 Use a hook knife to texture the curved outside part of each piece. This will take some time. With every grip, make sure your fingers are always out of the way of the blade.

FINISHING

8 Once both pieces have been textured, use a high-grit sandpaper (like 600) to smooth and refine the shape. Apply an oil or polyurethane finish and allow to dry.

SUCCULENT STAND

This stand is a simple and beautiful way to display not only succulents but any potted plant in a unique and eye-catching way. Make a thousand of these for your home!

HALF-DOME BASE

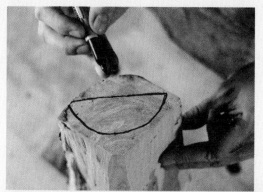

1 To get the required thickness for the base, it is best to start with a quartered log. A freshly split log is best, because it will be easier to do the carving that is necessary. Use a hatchet to remove the bark and pith. Mark a half-dome shape onto the end of the wood, then work down to that shape with the hatchet.

2 Use a compass to draw the largest diameter circle possible within the width of your log.

3 Use a saw to cut into the sides, beginning to define the shape of the half-dome. Then use the hatchet to rough out the underside of the half-dome shape. The goal here is to do the majority of the carving and shaping with the piece still attached to the log. This will keep you safe and your hands protected.

4 Use a straight knife to carve large facets into the underside of the piece; this will add some interest to the stand. Try to smooth out all of the surfaces as much as possible.

5 Once you have finished, separate the piece from the log using the saw. Clean off any saw marks with the knife.

LEGS

6 The three legs are positioned equidistant around the underside of the dome in the shape of a triangle. Mark and drill a hole for each leg, angling the holes by slightly tilting the drill away from the center.

7 Use a hatchet to split off three pieces from the remainder of the log. They should be of equal length and a thickness larger than the drill bit used for the holes in the dome.

8 Begin by shaping and fitting the ends into the holes on the underside of the dome. Start large and then take careful shavings to sneak up on a tight fit. Carve the other ends down to a taper.

FINISHING

9 Lightly sand all of the pieces and then glue the legs in place. You may need to shave a little off the bottom of one or two of the legs in order to get the succulent stand to sit level. Oil as desired.

COATRACK

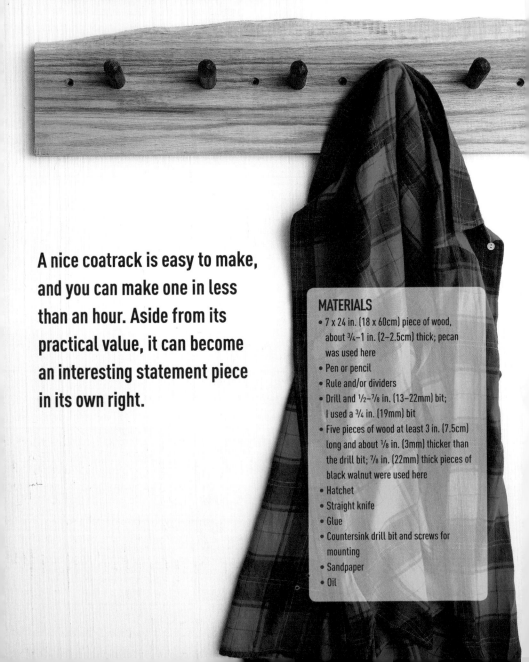

A nice coatrack is easy to make, and you can make one in less than an hour. Aside from its practical value, it can become an interesting statement piece in its own right.

MATERIALS
- 7 x 24 in. (18 x 60cm) piece of wood, about ¾–1 in. (2–2.5cm) thick; pecan was used here
- Pen or pencil
- Rule and/or dividers
- Drill and ½–⅞ in. (13–22mm) bit; I used a ¾ in. (19mm) bit
- Five pieces of wood at least 3 in. (7.5cm) long and about ⅛ in. (3mm) thicker than the drill bit; ⅞ in. (22mm) thick pieces of black walnut were used here
- Hatchet
- Straight knife
- Glue
- Countersink drill bit and screws for mounting
- Sandpaper
- Oil

BACK BOARD

1 Begin by drawing a centerline down the length of the wooden board. Divide the line into six equal parts, using a rule and math or a pair of dividers. There should be a mark every 4 in. (10cm) to indicate where the holes will be drilled for the five pegs.

2 Drill a hole at each mark, with the drill slightly angled so that the pegs will tilt upward. If you lock the drill against your body with your hand, you can get a fairly accurate and repeatable angle for each hole. Take care not to drill all the way through the wood and out the other side.

PEGS

3 Cut the five pieces of wood for the pegs to the same length and round their ends by knocking off the corners with a hatchet, taking care not to go smaller than the holes you have drilled. You can use a scrap piece of wood with a hole drilled in it to help you get the right size.

4 With a straight knife, use a chest-lever grip to continue rounding the pegs. Remember that a square stalk is made round by knocking off corners, moving from 4 sides to 8 sides, 8 to 16, 16 to 32, and so on—this will enable you to fit a square peg into a round hole.

5 After every few cuts, check the peg against the hole until it fits tightly. It is always better to start slightly oversized and sneak up on your fit with light shavings. As the old woodwork saying goes, "You can always take away wood but you can never put it back." Continue to carve and fit all five pegs.

6 If the pegs are longer than they need to be, go ahead and cut them to length and refine the shape by rounding over the ends with the knife. Once finished, glue them in place.

7 To give the board a little more visual interest, I created a faux "live" edge by chopping an irregular angle along the top edge. Carve out any hatchet marks with the knife. Doing this at the end will help you keep the coatrack looking in proportion and the pegs centered.

8 Using a countersink bit, drill four holes along the centerline—two on the outside and two in the middle. This is how you will attach the rack to the wall.

9 Sand lightly, oil as desired, and mount to the wall.

DOOR HANDLE

This is an easy project to make but carries a big effect. You can give an old dresser or tired kitchen new life with this quick and simple idea.

MATERIALS

- 1½ x 1½ x 9 in. (4 x 4 x 23cm) piece of wood; cherry was used here
- Hatchet
- Pen or pencil
- Saw
- Straight knife
- Machine screw with coarse thread
- Drill and drill bit same size or slightly smaller than barrel of screw (excluding width of threads)
- Screwdriver
- Sandpaper (optional)
- Oil

BASIC SHAPE

1 Round off the edges of the wood by removing all the corners with a hatchet, creating a somewhat octagonal cylinder. Draw a line about two fingers' width from the end; this establishes the maximum depth of the door handle. Draw the sloping sides of the handle on either side.

2 Saw a quarter of the way into the wood on all sides. Take care not to saw all the way through because you want the middle to remain attached to the long end of the wood. This gives you something to hold onto while you carve.

3 Use a straight knife to repeat these cuts about ½ in. (13mm) away from the first ones, cutting at an angle into the first saw cuts in order to take out a small wedge with each cut.

FACETS

4 Using a chest-lever grip, round off the end of the handle by taking off large facets. Switch to a thumb-lever grip to round off the end.

5 With the top finished, round off the underside with the knife. Once the majority of the work is done, use a saw to cut the handle away from the length of wood. Clean up any stray wood with the knife. You are now ready to make the hole to fix the handle to the door or drawer.

SCREW FIXING

6 For a wooden door handle, it is a good idea to use machine screws with a coarse thread. The slightly larger thread will bite into the wood and prevent it from stripping out during use. The drill bit should be the same size or slightly smaller than the barrel of the screw, not including the width of the threads. This can easily be checked by placing the drill bit over the screw to compare.

7 Secure the door handle to your workbench and drill a hole as vertical as possible about halfway into the wood. It is helpful to make a small mark with a pen or pencil on the side of the handle to indicate the stopping depth.

8 Use a screwdriver to insert the screw into the drilled hole.

FINISHING

9 Sand if desired and apply an oil finish. To install, simply unscrew the screw, place the handle on the front of the door, and reinsert the screw from the inside of the door.

DESK ORGANIZER

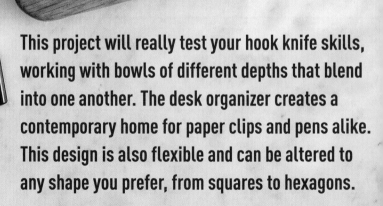

This project will really test your hook knife skills, working with bowls of different depths that blend into one another. The desk organizer creates a contemporary home for paper clips and pens alike. This design is also flexible and can be altered to any shape you prefer, from squares to hexagons.

BASIC SHAPE

1 Mark a rough 8 x 8 in. (20 x 20cm) square with a centerline running in one direction. Mark ⅜ in. (1cm) either side of the centerline at the top and ¾ in. (2cm) in from each corner on the bottom edge. Join the marks to form an open-ended triangle, then draw curves to form the points of the triangle. Draw a long, cylinder-like bowl at the bottom of the triangle and a small circle at the top. Join these at the center with a large circle that overlaps the other two bowls.

2 Use a tenon saw to cut out the triangle, cutting the points flat.

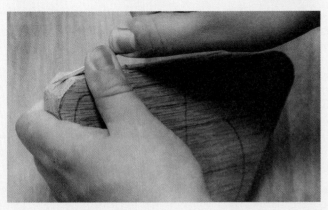

3 Use a straight knife to carve the points of the triangle into curves. Use thumb-lever cuts mostly, although chest-lever cuts will be useful if you have a larger amount of wood to remove.

4 Cut bevels along the edges of the triangle on both sides.

BOWLS

5 Switch to a hook knife to carve the top and bottom bowls, cutting across the grain and working from the center out. The top and bottom bowls will be deeper than the center bowl. As you carve, press your thumbs into the bowl to check that the depth is level.

6 Carve the center bowl last. The top and bottom bowls will give you somewhere to get purchase with your thumb while you do this. You can also try using the hook knife in a similar way to the chest-lever technique, cutting across the full width of the bowl rather than from the center outward. Carve carefully at the edge of the center bowl, being mindful not to cut into the other bowls. Take a moment before each cut to consider what you want to cut next.

FINISHING

7 Sand the whole piece, starting with 60–80 grit and working gradually through higher grits. Soak the wood under running water and allow to dry between every few grits. This will raise the grain and give a smoother, longer lasting finish to the organizer.

8 Apply oil or wax to finish. When dry, buff lightly with a cloth to bring the wood to a shine.

COMB

A lovely gift or a keepsake, this comb is simple to make. Remember to take your time when carving the teeth, as this is the most fragile part of the process and it is easy to cut away too much wood at this point.

MATERIALS
- ¼ x 3 x 3½ in. (0.6 x 7.5 x 9cm) piece of wood; oak was used here
- Hatchet (if using green wood)
- Pen or pencil
- Rule
- Compass
- Coping saw
- Straight knife
- Hook knife
- Sandpaper
- Oil or wax
- Cloth

BASIC SHAPE

1 If using green wood, use a hatchet to split a longer piece to around ¼ in. (5–8mm) thick; this will give you something to grip while carving. Measure and mark intervals of 1½, 2½, and 3½ in. (4, 8, and 9cm) from the end of the wood, making sure the direction of the grain runs down the length of the marked section. Mark a centerline through the middle of the comb and use a compass to create a curve in the ⅜ in. (1cm) section.

2 Use a coping saw to cut around the curve; this forms the top of the comb. Measure five tines in the bottom section; these will form the teeth of the comb. Mark the center and edge teeth first, and then add the final two between these. The tips should be around ⅛ in. (3–4mm) thick. Saw out the wood from between the teeth.

3 Use a straight knife and the chest-lever cutting technique to apply slight bevels around the edges of the comb. Continue to add bevels until a rounded edge begins to form. On the very top, apply a single bevel to the front and rear edges to remove the fragile right angles.

TEETH

4 Carve a taper into the teeth end of the comb, so that it angles in toward the tips of the teeth. A chest-lever cut is the quickest way to do this but also the riskiest. If you are not yet confident with this cut, taking your time with a thumb-lever cut will do this perfectly, too.

5 Using a thumb-lever cut, round off the teeth of the comb, shaping both the inside edges and the tip of the teeth. Use the very tip of the knife to make small, precise cuts and reduce the risk of cutting too much wood.

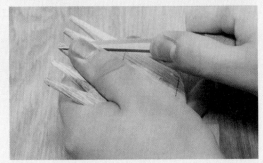

HANDLE

6 Mark a small circle on either side of the centerline, then join them with lines at the top and bottom to create an oval. You can draw the oval freehand if you prefer, but the circles will help you to line everything up symmetrically. Do this on both sides of the comb.

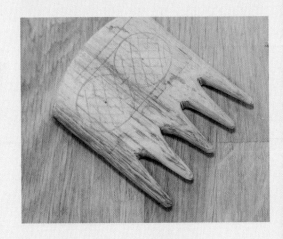

7 Use a hook knife to carve small hollows in the marked ovals. These indentations will act as a nest for the thumb and fingers when using the comb. They do not need to be very deep, barely $1/16$ in. (1–2mm).

FINISHING

8 Sand the comb, starting with 60–80 grit and working gradually through higher grits. To sand between the teeth, roll the sandpaper into a cylinder to get better access. After every few grits, soak the comb under running water and allow to dry before moving on to the next grit. This will raise the grain of the wood and provide a smoother finish.

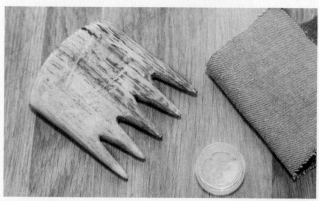

9 Apply an oil or wax finish to bring out the pattern in the grain. Once dry, buff the comb lightly with a cloth to bring the wood to a shine.

MATERIALS

- 3¼ x 4¾ in. (8 x 12cm) piece of wood, ⅜–⅝ in. (1–1.5cm) thick; redwood was used here
- Pen or pencil
- Rule
- Tenon saw
- Compass
- Straight knife
- Hook knife
- Sandpaper
- Oil or wax
- Cloth

PINCH POT

Pinch pots are a lovely project
for using up smaller pieces of wood,
and offer a good chance to practice your cutting
techniques before moving on to more intricate projects.

BASIC SHAPE

1 Mark diagonal lines across the corners of the wood, ¾ in. (2cm) in from each edge. Saw off the corners to leave you with a gemstone shape.

2 Mark a centerline across the wood, then use a compass to draw two 1 in. (2.5cm) diameter circles on this line. The edge of each circle should be at least ⅜ in. (1cm) in from the short sides of the wood.

3 Mark a line ¼ in. (5mm) in from the edges to indicate the bevel. Using a straight knife and thumb-lever cuts, carve the bevel around the top edge. For the longer edges, you could also use a chest-lever cut. Repeat the process on the underside but make the bevel a little smaller.

BOWLS

4 Switch to a hook knife and carve out the two bowls, cutting across the grain to avoid catching the wood. To keep your thumb away from the cutting path of the knife, tuck it as far under the piece as you can while maintaining control of the wood. Carve each bowl to approximately the same depth; they should be less than ¼ in. (5mm) at the deepest point.

FINISHING

5 Sand the wood, starting with 60–80 grit and working gradually through higher grits. Soak the wood under running water after every few grits and allow to dry before continuing to sand; this will raise the grain and give you a smoother finish.

6 Use a food-safe oil or wax to season and seal the wood. After the finish has dried, buff the wood lightly with a cloth to bring out the shine.

PAN TRIVET

MATERIALS

- 8 x 8 in. (20 x 20cm) piece of wood (or size to suit your pan), $\frac{1}{2}$–$\frac{3}{4}$ in. (1.5–2cm) thick; poplar was used here
- Pen or pencil
- Rule
- Compass
- Coping saw
- Straight knife
- Hook knife
- Drill and $\frac{5}{16}$–$\frac{3}{8}$ in. (8–10mm) bit
- Sandpaper
- Oil or wax
- Cloth

This pan trivet will make a wonderful addition to your kitchen, celebrating the beautiful patterns in the wood grain in an elegant, modern design.

BASIC SHAPE

1 Using a square of wood to suit your pan size, mark a centerline running across the square in each direction, dividing the wood into quarters.

2 Make a small mark ¾ in. (2cm) to either side of each centerline at the edge of the wood. Press the point of a compass as close as possible into one corner of the wood. Open the compass so that the other point touches one of the nearest small marks and draw a quarter circle; it should roughly join up a pair of the small marks. Repeat this at each corner.

3 Open the compass around ¼ in. (5mm) wider and mark quarter circles from each corner as before. These lines will act as a guide for carving the bevels.

4 Use a coping saw to cut along the outermost of each pair of curved lines, removing the excess wood and leaving you with the basic shape of the trivet.

5 Using a straight knife and chest-lever cuts, clean up any wobbles from the saw cutting and then carve the bevels. A thumb-lever cut will be more useful for beveling the very end sections. Keep an eye on the direction of the grain; sometimes you may need to cut from the center of the curve outward, while at other times from the end of the curve inward. Take your first passes gently; if the wood resists, try a different direction.

6 Draw a large circle in the center of the trivet and then use a hook knife to hollow it out to a depth of about ⅛ in. (2–3mm). Make sure the knife is sharp and try to make long, smooth cuts. The cut marks can add interest to the finished trivet, but if you prefer, you can sand this section smooth instead and the polished wood will still look glorious.

7 Flip the wood over to the other side of the trivet and mark the two centerlines as before. Draw a 2–2½ in. (5–6cm) diameter circle in the center and then a semicircle at each end of the cross shape to form the feet.

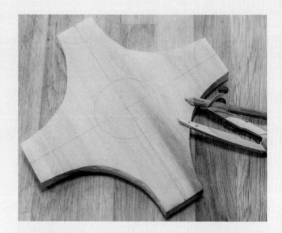

8 Carve away about ³⁄₁₆ in. (4–5mm) from the space between the feet and center circle. Use the straight knife where possible, as this will give a smoother finish and make sanding a much easier task. If certain sections are tough to access with a straight blade, you can use the hook knife instead.

9 You will be left with four raised feet and a raised center section. Rest the trivet on its feet and check for wobbles (seasoned wood can sometime have a little warping; green wood usually has a little difference somewhere). Carve thin layers off the feet until any wobbles are gone.

10 Drill five holes in a cross pattern in the center of the trivet. I used a ³/₈ in. (10mm) bit for the center hole and a ⁵/₁₆ in. (8mm) bit for the outer holes, but the size does not matter.

FINISHING

11 Avoiding the center, sand the edge of the trivet starting with a low grit like 60 or 80 and gradually working up to higher grits. To keep the cut marks in the center, use emery paper (also known as silicon carbide paper or wet/dry paper) and begin with a very high grit (like 400). If you used a very sharp blade for your carving, the cuts should already be very smooth, but they may need some sanding in a few spots. Use a fingertip to sand gently into each cut, working in the direction it was made.

12 Apply a finish of oil or wax to bring out the detail in the grain and protect the piece. Once dry, buff lightly with a cloth to bring out the shine.

OFFCUT CAR

The term "offcut" refers to any piece of wood that is cut off the end of a project piece. With a little imagination, these scrap pieces can be transformed into a fun carving project and make great toys that kids love.

MATERIALS

- Piece of scrap wood; black walnut was used here
- Two short lengths of dowel, one ³/₈–½ in. (1–1.5cm) thick for the axles and the other 1 in. (2.5cm) thick or larger for the wheels (or use scrap wood for the wheels)
- Saw
- Pen or pencil
- Straight knife
- Hook knife
- Drill and drill bit slightly larger than thickness of axle dowel
- Glue
- Sandpaper
- Oil

BODY AND AXLES

1 Start with a small piece of scrap wood. You can saw a piece off an existing board or dig through your scrap bin for something suitable. Roughly draw the side profile of the car onto the wood. Mark two holes for where the wheels will go.

2 Use a straight knife to round off the top corners, and then use a hook knife to add a bit of texture by lightly carving the sides.

3 Redraw the holes if necessary, then drill straight through the wood using a drill bit that is slightly larger than the axle dowel. This will give the wheels room to spin.

4 Insert the dowel and cut two pieces long enough to protrude about 1 in. (2.5cm) on both sides of the car.

WHEELS

5 If you are not using store-bought dowel for the wheels, you can carve your own by rounding off a thicker scrap piece of wood. Start with a square piece and cut off the corners until it is round—work from 4 corners to 8, 8 corners to 16, and so on.

6 Secure the wheel dowel firmly to your workbench and drill vertically through the center as deep as necessary to make four wheels. Saw off four equal slices.

ASSEMBLY

7 Glue a wheel to one side of each axle. When dry, insert the axles into the car, leaving a little space between the wheel and car. Add a small amount of glue to the other end of each axle and attach the remaining wheels.

8 After the glue has dried, saw off the excess dowel.

9 Sand off any rough edges, oil as desired, and the car is ready to play with.

LOVE SPOON

This spoon builds on the skills you practiced for the cooking spoon, using a hook knife for the concave surface of the bowl. However, the decorative elements of the hearts on the handle of the spoon are more intricate, allowing you to take your whittling skills to the next level.

MATERIALS

- Piece of wood 6¾–8 in. (17–20cm) long, at least 2–2½ in. (5–6cm) wide, and ½ in. (12–15mm) thick; iroko was used here
- Pen or pencil
- Rule
- Compass
- Coping saw
- Straight knife
- Hook knife
- Drill and 5/16–3/8 in. (8–10mm) bit
- Sandpaper
- Oil or wax
- Cloth

BASIC SHAPE

1 Mark a centerline down the length of the wood and draw the bowl shape at one end. This one is a shield-style shape, but you can draw an egg shape or circle if you prefer. Its height should be 2–2½ in. (5–6cm), which is around a third of the length of the spoon.

2 Divide the handle into thirds lengthwise, then the top third in half again. Draw a large heart around the middle third of the handle. It should be about as wide as the bowl. Add curved lines to connect the heart with the bowl. It may be helpful to draw lines parallel to the centerline at ¼ in. (5mm) intervals to line everything up. In the top two sections of the handle, draw a smaller heart above the large heart with a rounded section at the top.

3 Use a coping saw to cut carefully around the outline of the spoon. Where there are tight angles, you may need to cut in from various directions. Take your time. A smooth cut is far easier to work with later, even if it is off the line a little, so make corrections gently; sudden changes of direction will be difficult to work with later.

BACK OF BOWL

4 Mark the depth of the bowl on the sides of the wood and indicate the waste that needs to be cut away from the back of the bowl.

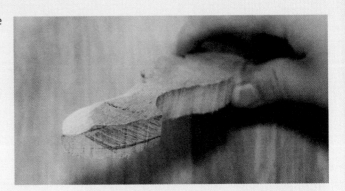

5 Use the saw to cut the basic shape for the back of the bowl. This can also be done using a knife and the chest-lever technique, but this is both riskier and harder work, particularly if using a tougher wood. Cut the diagonals first and then the center to reduce how much wood you are cutting at any one time.

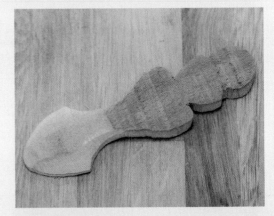

6 Use a straight knife to work on the back of the bowl and the lowest section of the handle; you will most likely have cut one side slightly differently from the other with the saw, so use the knife and thumb-lever cuts to balance it out and get the shape you want. Use the chest-lever technique if you need to remove larger amounts of wood; use the tip of the knife and make the cut almost in slow motion if you need extra control.

HANDLE

7 To make the "step" at the bottom of the first heart, use chest-lever cuts to carve repeatedly in one direction up to the edge of the heart. Switch to thumb-lever cuts to remove any feathers that form and finish the step.

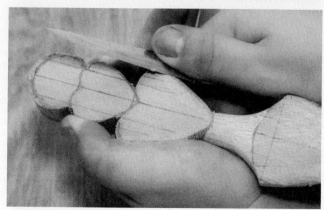

8 Begin shaping the larger of the two hearts, combining chest-lever and thumb-lever cuts to curve the edges into a rounded heart. Concentrate on the front face for now.

9 Continue this process, working in turn on the smaller heart and the rounded section at the top of the handle.

10 On the reverse of the spoon, carve small steps between the two hearts and the round tip, but keep the bowl and handle running smoothly into the first heart to help keep plenty of strength in that section.

INSIDE OF BOWL

11 Use a hook knife to carve the bowl of the spoon, working from the center out and across the grain and carving the full width of the bowl before going deeper. This will help you make longer, smoother cuts and keep the bowl level throughout.

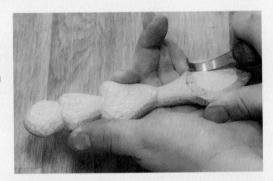

FINISHING

12 Drill a hole in the top of the spoon. It is important to make a smaller guiding hole first to avoid the drill bit catching and risking damage to the spoon. Start sanding with a low grit like 60 or 80 and work through to higher grits. Soak the wood under running water and allow to dry between every few grits; this will raise the grain and give a smoother finish. Apply oil or wax, allow to dry, then buff lightly with a cloth to bring out the shine.

AIRPLANE

A beautiful hand-carved toy, this plane will thrill your kids or make a fantastic gift. The textured surface is great for sensory development, and the untreated wood is safe for small hands and mouths.

PLANE BODY

1 Use a hatchet to split the wood in half lengthwise. Set one half aside for the wings and use the other for the body. Draw the side profile of the airplane onto the 3 in. (7.5cm) wide face of the wood.

2 Use a saw to make a series of relief cuts along the edge and then carve down to the drawn lines with the hatchet.

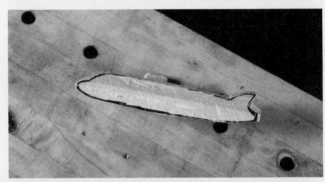

3 Draw a centerline along the top of the plane's body and use this to help you sketch out two matching tapers from nose to tail. Use a straight knife and power cuts to shape both of the tapers.

4 Now begin removing the corners, using long cuts to get smooth, continuous surfaces. Work along the length of the plane, changing shape from a square to an octagon, then from 8 sides to 16 and so on.

5 Use a thumb-lever grip to make cuts into the open space above your thumb to round off the nose. Switch to a hook knife to cut the transition from the tail fin to the body. Finish with the straight knife to give the plane a long and relatively flat belly. Smooth the transitions from the bottom into the sides.

WINGS

6 Use the hatchet to cut a ¼ in. (5mm) thick by 2½ in. (6cm) wide piece from the remaining half of the wood. Keep checking the length of the wood to make sure you are cutting straight. This will also reveal any curving or overly deep cuts.

7 Place the body of the plane on top of the wing section and use it to mark the length of the wings. The wings should be as wide as the plane is long; anything longer or shorter looks odd to the eye. Cut off any excess.

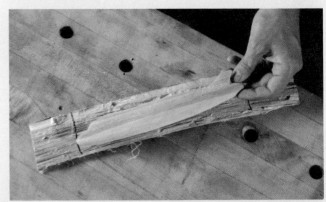

8 Place the wing section on an outstretched finger and mark the middle, where it balances. Place the plane body on top of the wing section, centered over the middle mark. Then mark the width of the plane body onto the wing section. Using the straight knife, carve the rear of the wings straight and the front at an angle, starting at the point where you marked the plane's width and extending to the wingtips. Round off the wingtips.

9 Place the wings onto the underside of the plane, and mark the front and back of the wing section onto the plane. Saw along both marks on the plane body to the same depth as the wings. These cuts establish the depth of the slot that the wing section will sit in, flush to the plane body.

10 Carve out the slot, starting at the saw cuts and then removing the high spot in the middle. Make sure the bottom is flat. Next check that the wings will fit, using the straight knife to take very careful shavings off the front and back of the wing section if necessary. Check the fit after each cut. It is very easy to take off too much and to be left with loose wings.

11 Place a little glue into the slot and onto the wings where they meet the body. Clamp them together if possible, or just squeeze them together for 5–10 minutes until they feel secure. Once the glue dries, drill a little hole through the center of the wings and into the body, then insert a wooden dowel to hold everything together. Cut the dowel flush with the wings for a neat finish.

RESOURCES

US & CANADA

Council Tools
www.counciltool.com;
made-in-the-US tool
specialist

Hatchets and Axes
www.hatchetsandaxes.com;
hatchet, axe, and knife
specialist

Highland Woodworking
www.highlandwoodworking.
com; wide selection of
whittling and carving tools

Home Depot
www.homedepot.com; large
home improvement retailer

Lee Valley Tools
www.leevalley.com;
woodworking tool specialist
based in Canada

Lowe's
www.lowes.com; large home
improvement retailer

*Peachtree Woodworking
Supply*
www.ptreeusa.com; wide
selection of hand tools

*Rockler Woodworking and
Hardware*
www.rockler.com; wide
selection of hand tools

Silky Saws
www.silkysaws.com; saw
specialist

Texas Knife
www.texasknife.com; knife
specialist based in Texas

True Value
www.truevalue.com; large
retailers' cooperative
hardware store

Woodcraft
www.woodcraft.com;
whittling supplies stockist
with 76 US stores; ships
worldwide

UK

B&Q
www.diy.com; large home
improvement retailer

Blades
www.blades.co.uk; hatchet,
axe, and knife supplier based
in Oldham

Classic Hand Tools
www.classichandtools.com;
woodworking tool specialist
based in Suffolk

Homebase
www.homebase.co.uk; large
home improvement retailer

Hunter's Knives
www.hunters-knives.co.uk;
hatchet, axe, and knife
supplier based in
Manchester

Saunders Seasonings
www.saunders-seasonings.
co.uk; wood specialist based
in London

Springfields
www.springfields.co.uk;
retailer of outdoor activity
tools, including a large
section on wood carving,
based in Burton

Wickes
www.wickes.co.uk; large
home improvement retailer

Wood Tools
www.wood-tools.co.uk;
small online woodwork tool
supplier

Woodshop Direct
www.woodshopdirect.co.uk;
wood specialists based in
Cornwall

Woodsmith Experience
www.woodsmithexperience.
co.uk; woodcraft school with
specialist shop

EDITORIAL NOTE

There are many fantastic tutorial videos online that show the
proper methods and movements of sharpening the specific
tools mentioned in this book. The best ones I would
recommend are by Ben Orford and Barn the Spoon.

INDEX

CREDITS

Josh Nava is a woodworker and project artisan for Global Outreach Developments Int'l, a development agency and school located in Nashville, TN, USA. He specializes in hand-crafted goods made from repurposed timber. In 2014 he completed the 365 Spoons Project where he documented the carving of a spoon everyday for a year.

Transcription and Writing Assistance: Deborah Nava

With special thanks to Vic Phillips for his work on the following projects: Desk organizer, Comb, Pinch pot, Pan trivet, and Love spoon

Vic Phillips, otherwise known as Single Malt Teapot, began carving in North London before heading to the Brecon Beacons in South Wales, where he now lives and crafts in the shadow of Pen Y Fan. Combining traditional, heritage crafting techniques and contemporary design leanings, Vic seeks to inspire his love of carving in those who may stumble across his work, and to encourage a connection to the long-grown stories on natural materials. He is also an emphatic nerd, a doting new father, and a lover of a good cake.

Photographers: Adam Loeffler, Gregg Garner, Joel Olson, Craig Duffy, Austin Bennecker, Canaan Kagay